Foodie Alphabet

Wynnie Au

DEDICATION

For Audrey

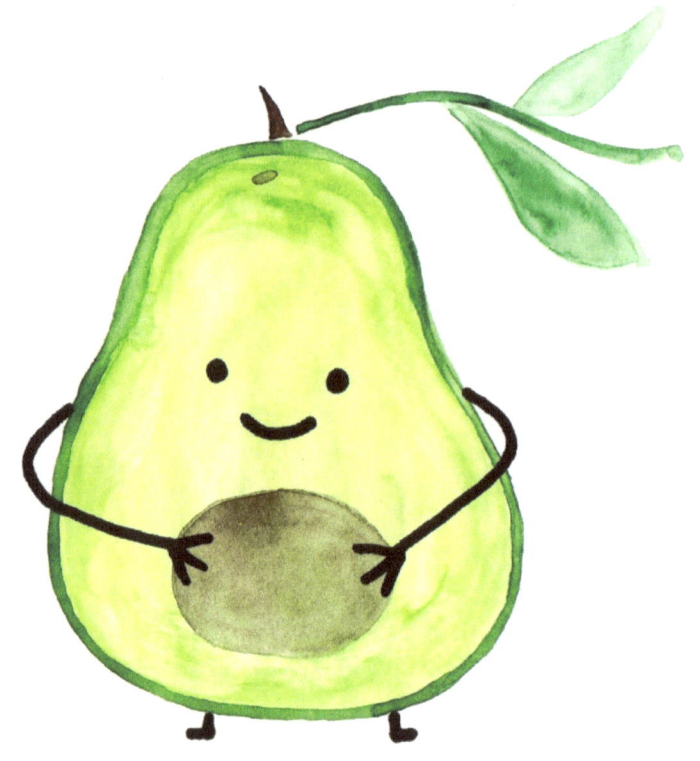

A is for Avocado

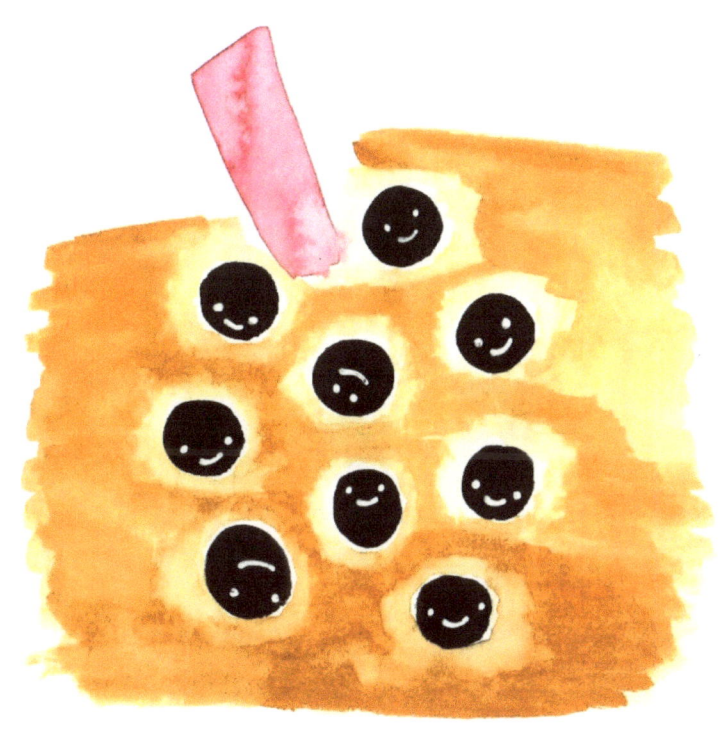

B is for Boba

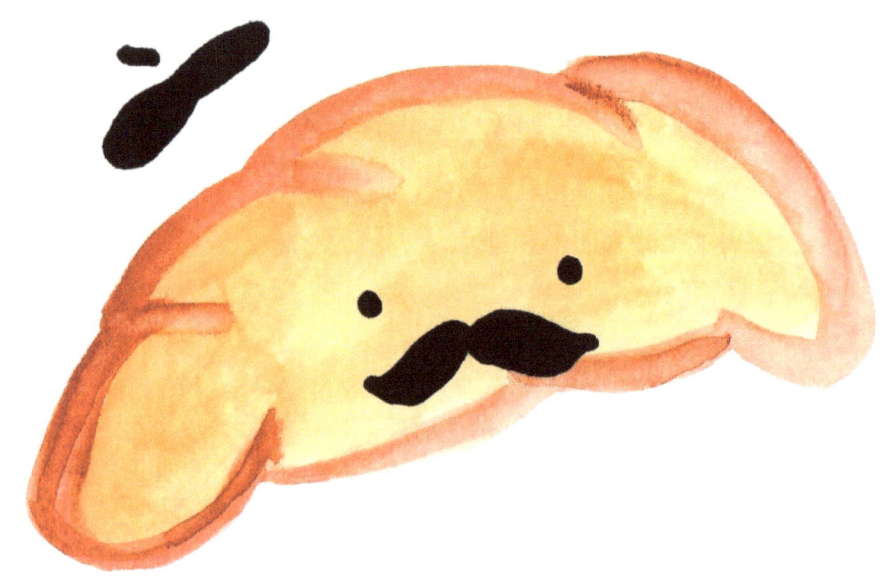

C is for Croissant

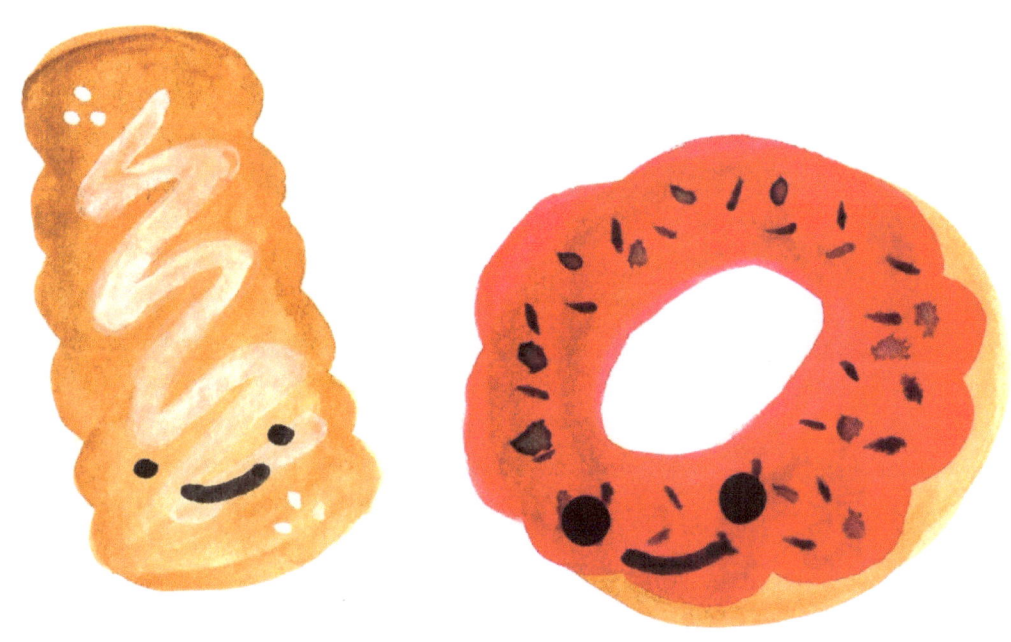

D is for Doughnut

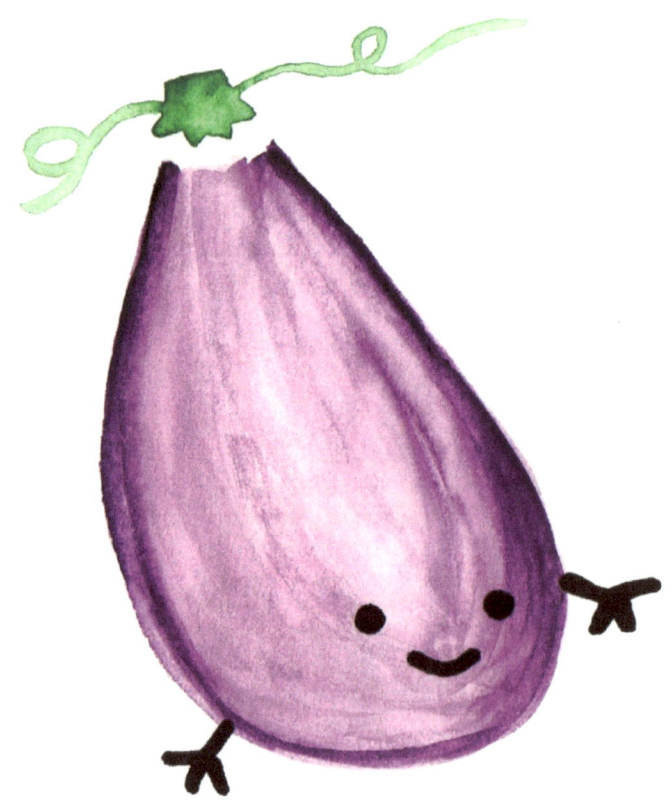

E is for Eggplant

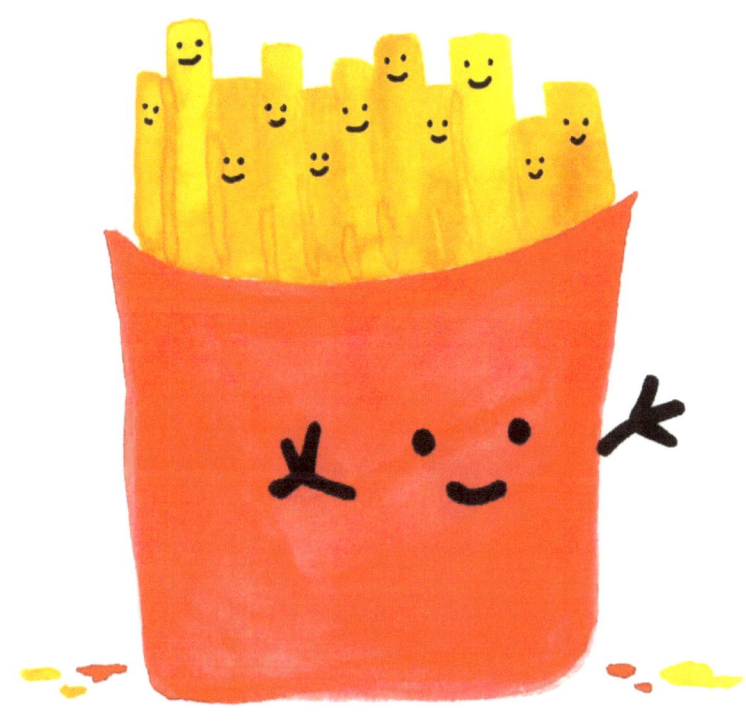

F is for Fries

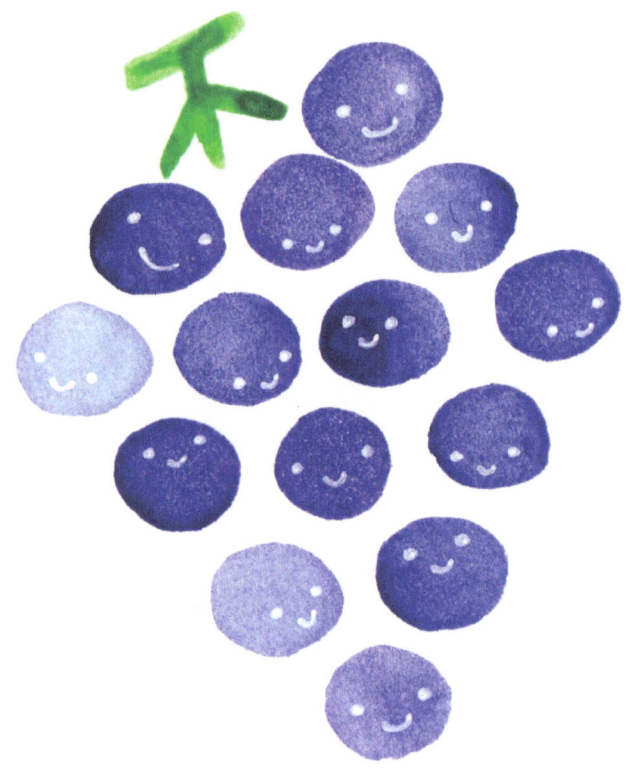

G is for Grapes

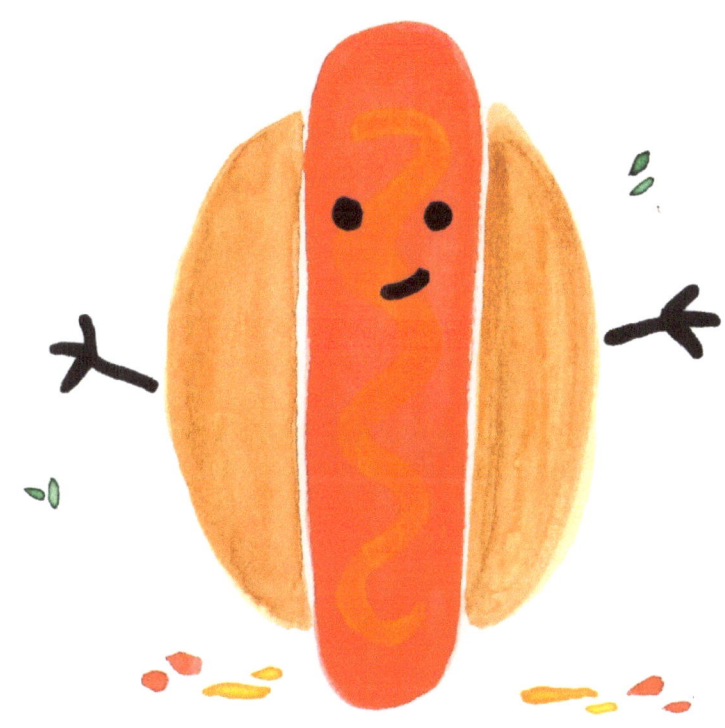

H is for Hot Dog

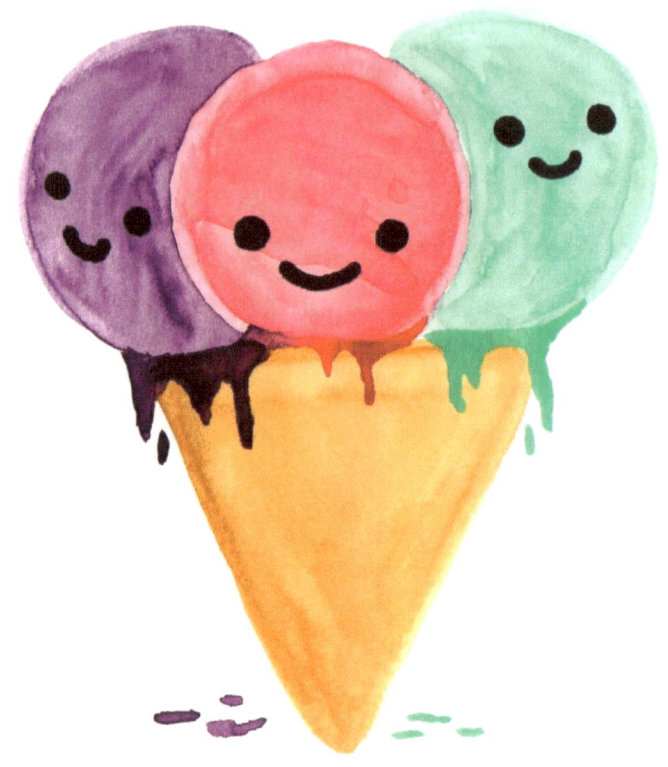

I is for Ice Cream

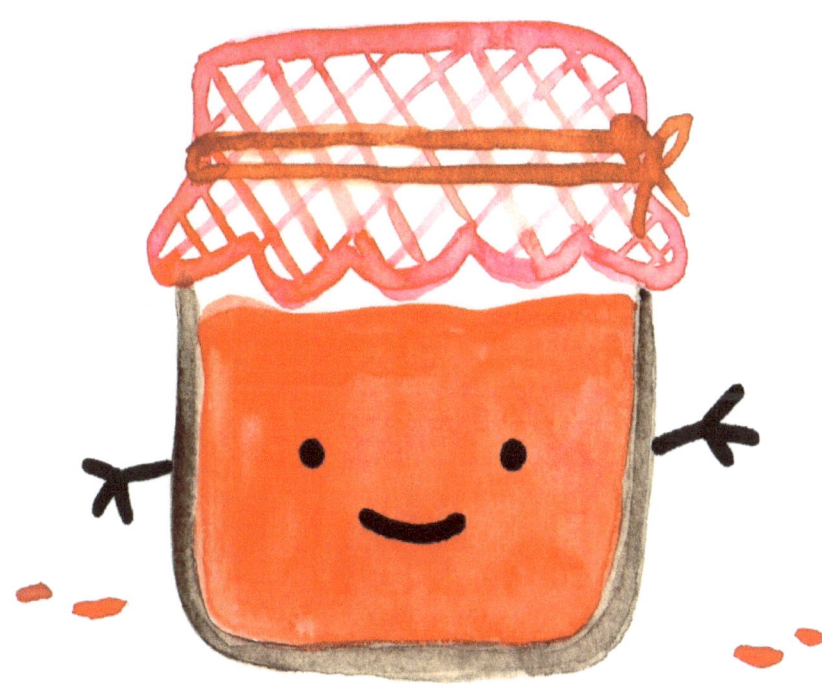

J is for Jam

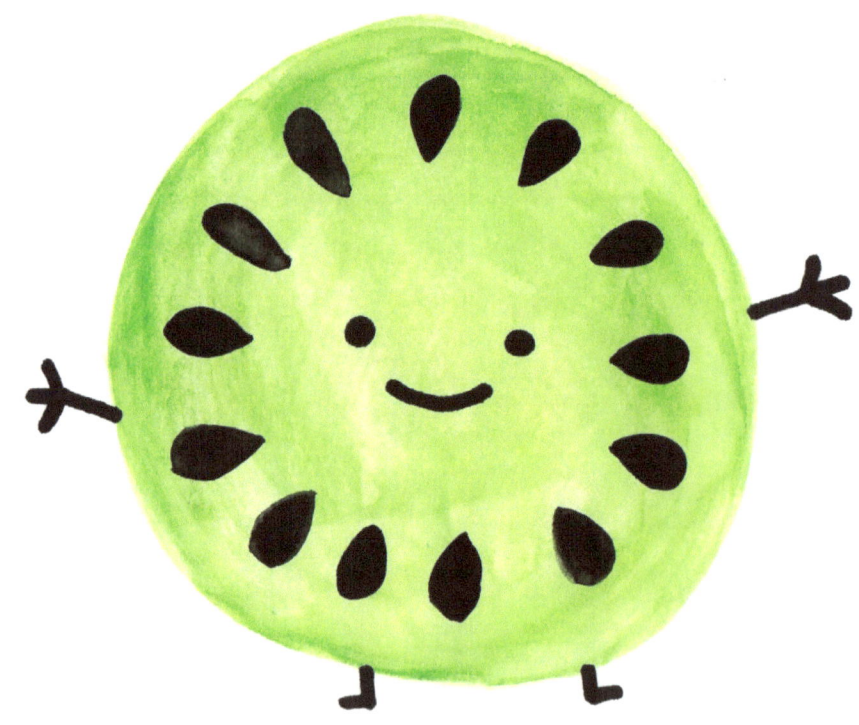

K is for Kiwi

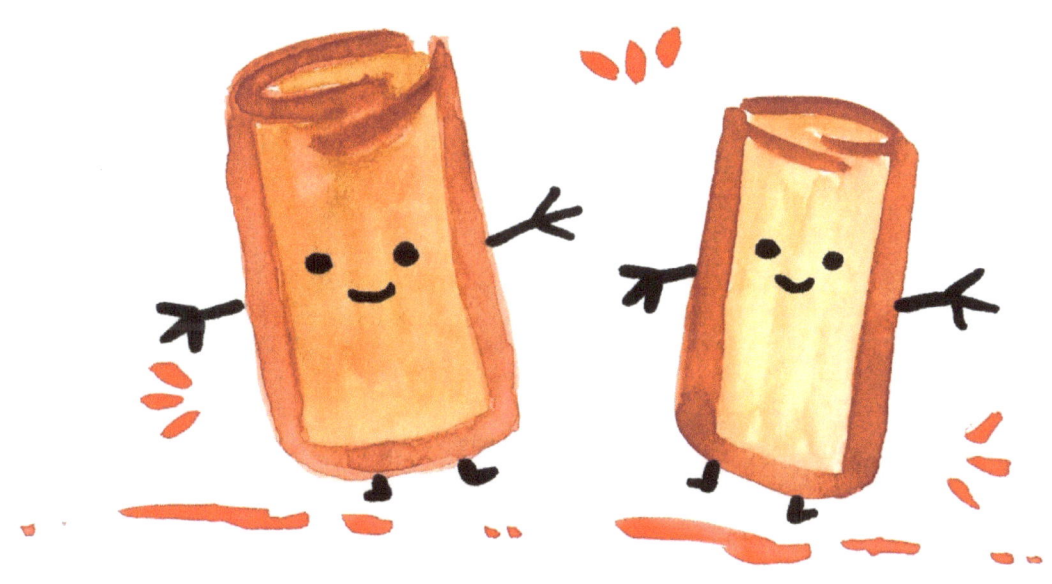

L is for Lumpia

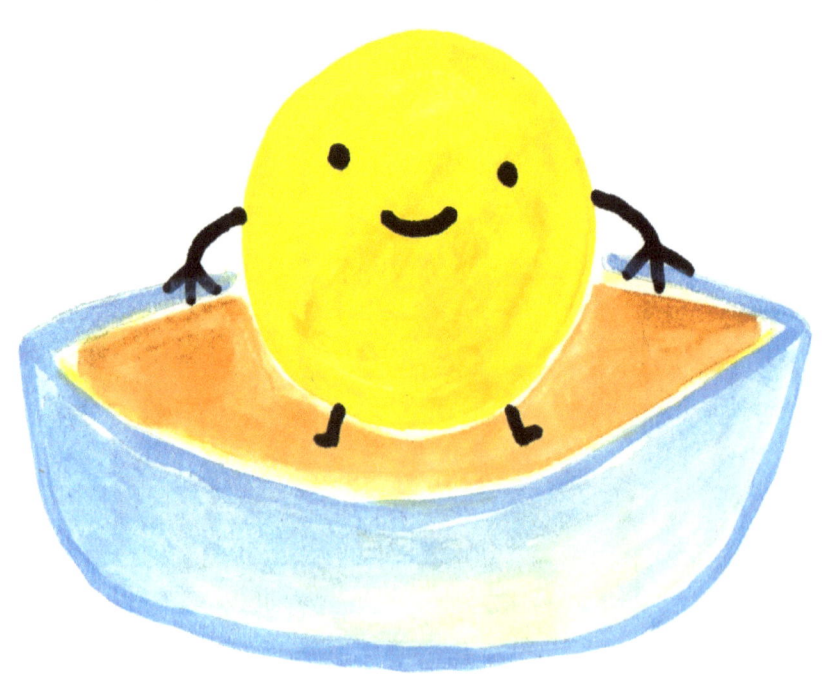

M is for Matzo Ball

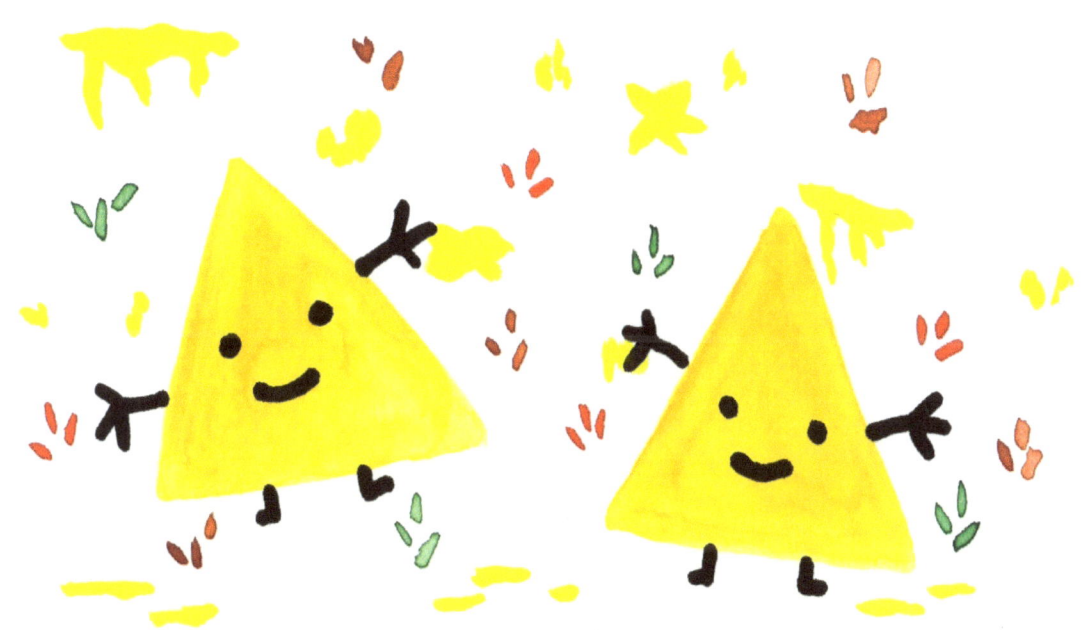

N is for Nachos

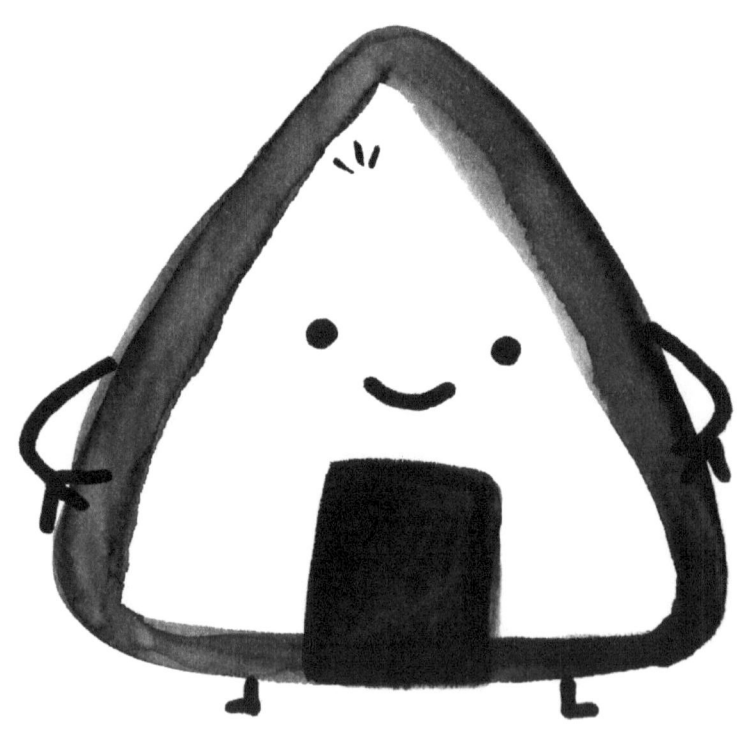

O is for Onigiri

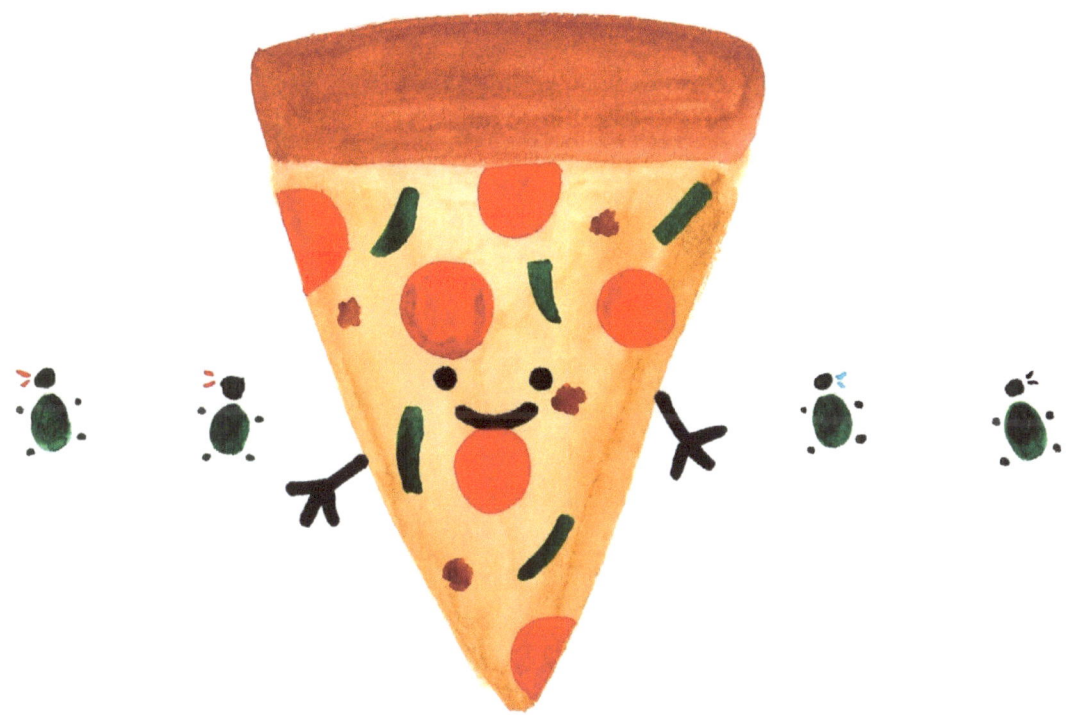

P is for Pizza

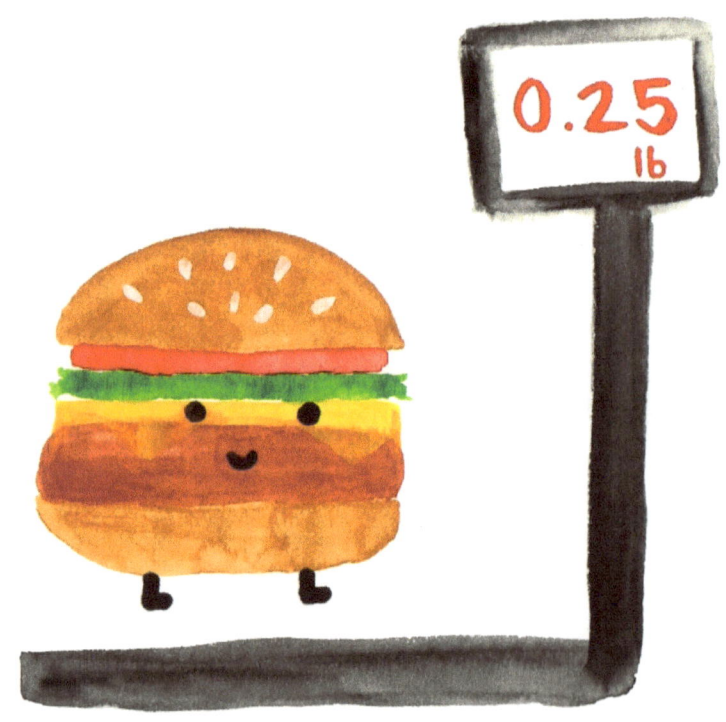

Q is for Quarter Pounder

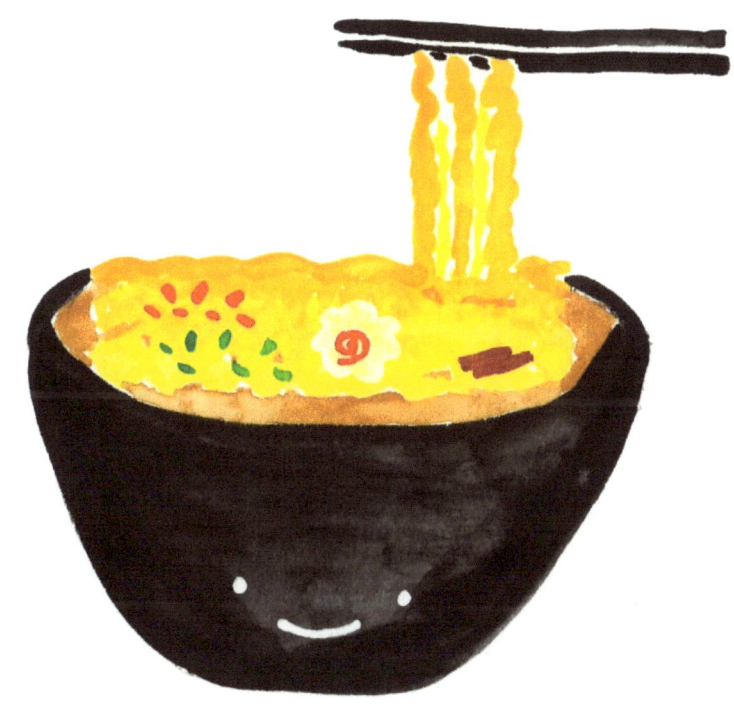

R is for Ramen

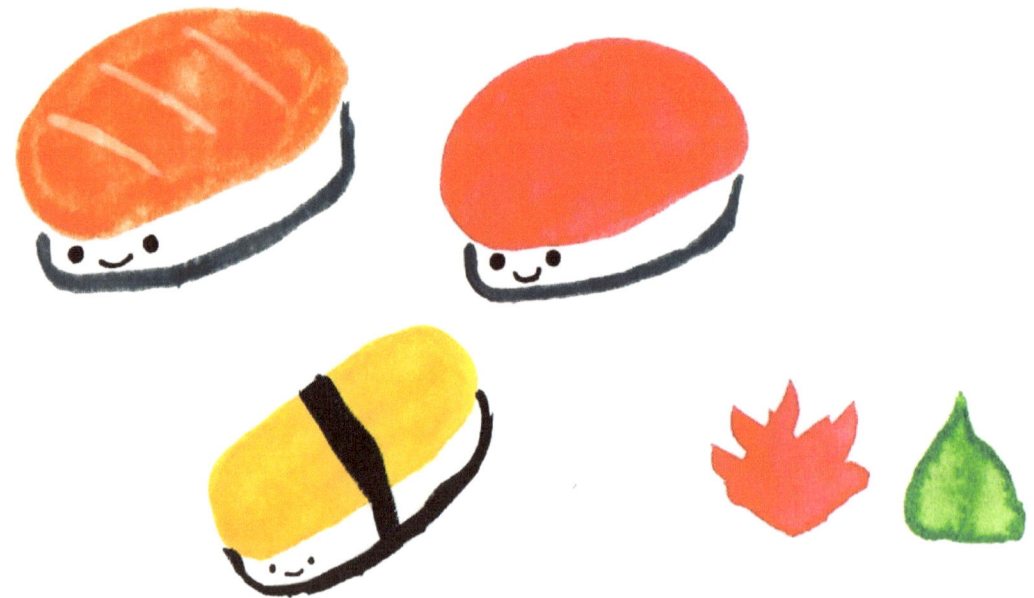

S is for Sushi

T is for Taco

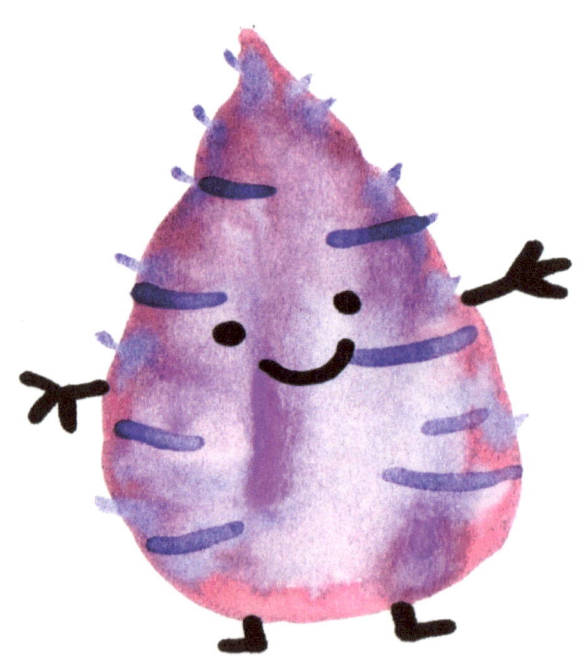

U is for Ube

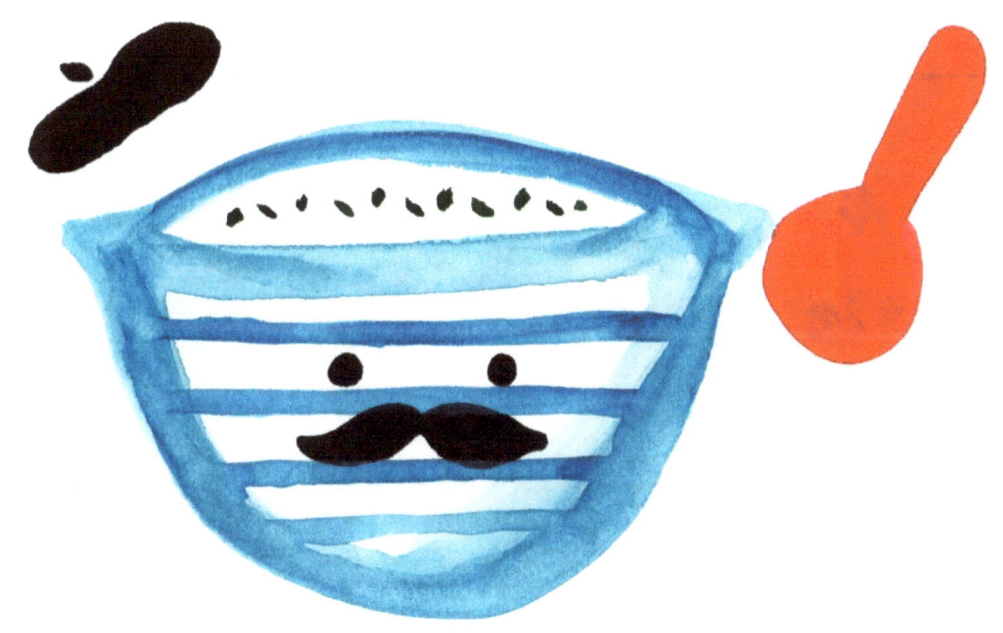

V is for Vichyssoise

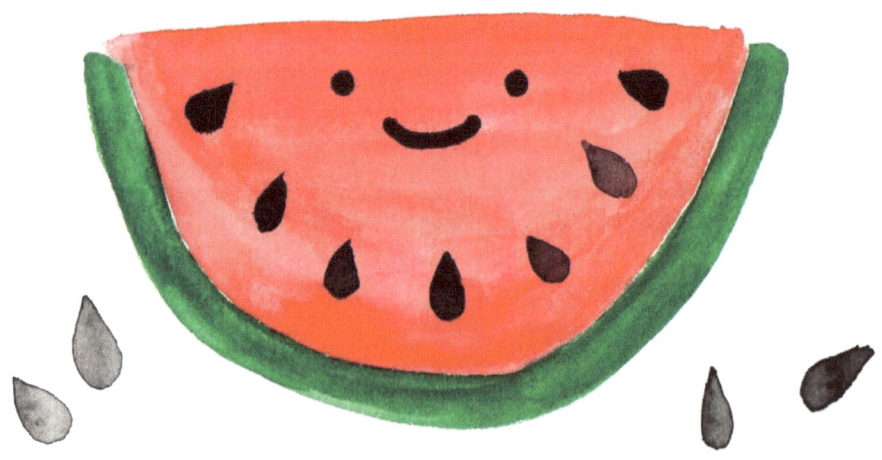

W is for Watermelon

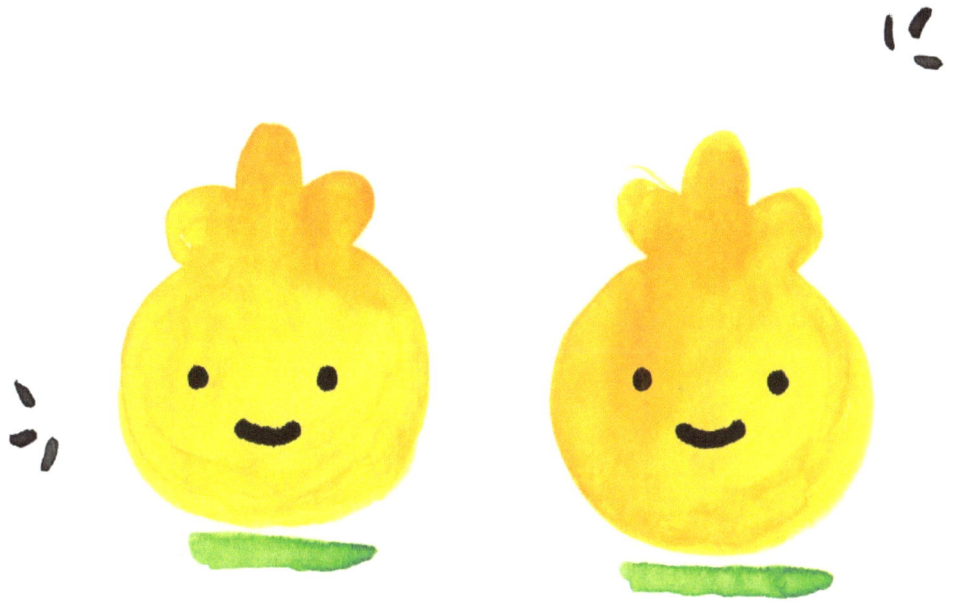

X is for Xiao Long Bao

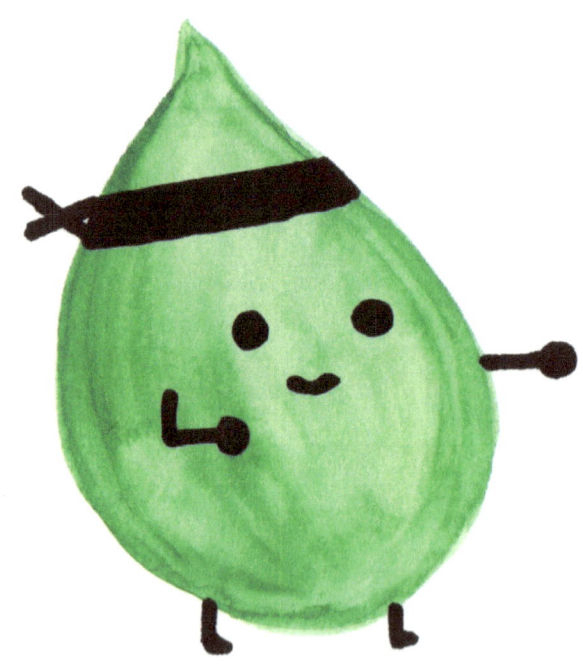

Y is for Yuzu

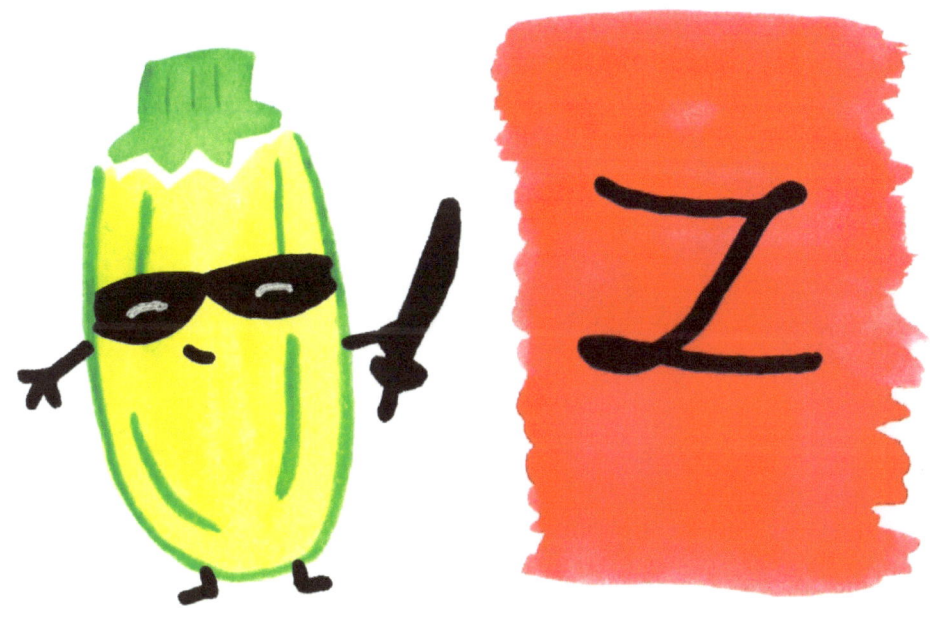

Z is for Zucchini